GIFTED
&
TALENTED®

*To develop
your child's gifts
and talents*

LANGUAGE ARTS

GIFTED
&
TALENTED®

*To develop
your child's gifts
and talents*

LANGUAGE ARTS

A Workbook for Ages 6–8

Written by Susan Amerikaner
Edited by Ann Laner and Helene Chirinian
Illustrated by Leesa Whitten
Designed by Zofia H. Kostyrko

Lowell House House
Juvenile
Los Angeles
CONTEMPORARY
BOOKS
Chicago

Manufactured in the United States of America

ISBN 1-56565-064-6

10 9 8 7 6 5 4

Cover design: Brenda Leach
Cover illustration: Kerry Manwaring

Note to Parents

GIFTED AND TALENTED WORKBOOKS will help develop your child's natural talents and gifts by providing activities to enhance critical and creative thinking skills. These skills of logic and reasoning teach children **how** to think. They are precisely the skills emphasized by teachers of gifted and talented children.

Thinking skills are the skills needed to be able to learn anything at any time. Unlike events, words, and teaching methods, thinking skills never change. If a child has a grasp of how to think, school success and even success in life will become more assured. In addition, the child will become self-confident as he or she approaches new tasks with the ability to think them through and discover solutions.

GIFTED AND TALENTED WORKBOOKS present these skills in a unique way, combining the basic subject areas of reading, language arts, and math with thinking skills. The top of each page is labeled to indicate the specific thinking skill developed. Here are some of the skills you will find:

- Deduction – the ability to reach a logical conclusion by interpreting clues

- Understanding relationships – the ability to recognize how objects, shapes, and words are similar or dissimilar; to classify and categorize

- Sequencing – the ability to organize events, numbers; to recognize patterns

- Inference – the ability to reach logical conclusions from given or assumed evidence

- Creative thinking – the ability to generate unique ideas; to compare and contrast the same elements in different situations; to present imaginative solutions to problems

How to Use Gifted & Talented Workbooks

Each book contains activities that challenge children. The activities vary in range from easier to more difficult. You may need to work with your child on many of the pages, especially with the child who is a non-reader. However, even a non-reader can master thinking skills, and the sooner your child learns how to think, the better. Read the directions to your child, and if necessary, explain them. Let your child choose to do the activities that interest him or her. When interest wanes, stop. A page or two at a time may be enough, as the child should have fun while learning.

It is important to remember that these activities are designed to teach your child **how to think,** not how to find the right answer. Teachers of gifted children are never surprised when a child discovers a new "right" answer. For example, a child may be asked to choose the object that doesn't belong in this group: a table, a chair, a book, a desk. The best answer is **book,** since all the others are furniture. But a child could respond that all of them belong because they all could be found in an office. The best way to react to this type of response is to praise the child and gently point out that there is another answer too. While creativity should be encouraged, your child must look for the best and most **suitable** answer.

GIFTED AND TALENTED WORKBOOKS have been written and designed by teachers. Educationally sound and endorsed by leaders in the gifted field, this series will benefit any child who demonstrates curiosity, imagination, a sense of fun and wonder about the world, and a desire to learn. These books will open your child's mind to new experiences and help fulfill his or her true potential.

Read all the clues. Write the correct letter on each pancake. Hint: Make sure you read all the clues before you start.

1. **J** is on top.

2. **P** is under **M**.

3. **U** is under **J**.

What word did you spell? _____

Read all the clues. Write the correct letter on each drum.

1. The first drum in the line is **H**.

2. **R** is behind **C**.

3. **M** is last.

4. **A** is between **R** and **M**.

What word did you spell? _____

Read all the clues. Write the correct letter in each space.

1. **H** is on the bottom.

2. **P** is not on top.

3. **S** is between **H** and **A**.

4. **L** is under **P**.

5. There is one more **S**.

What word did you spell? _____

Read all the clues. Write the correct letter on each hatbox.

1. One box is **A**.

2. **P** is the highest box.

3. **I** is between **P** and **R**.

4. **T** is not next to **R**.

5. **E** is on the bottom.

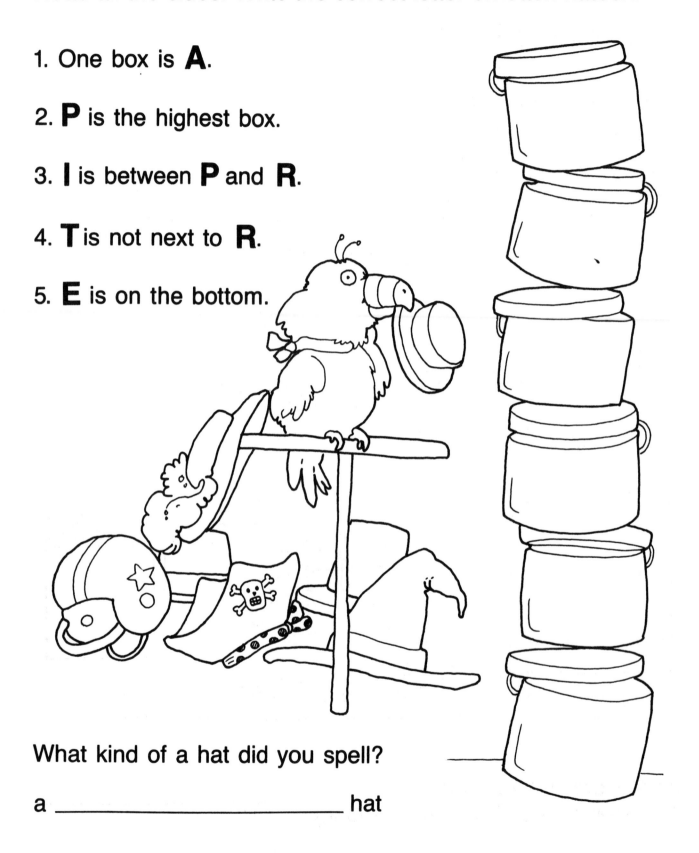

What kind of a hat did you spell?

a _____ hat

Read all the clues. Write the correct letter in each box.

1. The biggest box is **C**.
2. **C** is across from **Y**.
3. **A** is **not** next to **D**.
4. **A** is next to **N**.
5. **C** is **not** next to **D**.

What word did you spell?
(It's what Rosie Rhino loves most.) _____

Read all the clues. Write the correct letter in each car.

1. **D** is the biggest car.

2. **D** is between **E** and **R**.

3. **R** is behind **I**.

4. One car is **V**.

What word did you spell? (Start with the letter on the biggest car.) _____

Long ago Indians drew pictures to tell stories or send messages. Look at the Indian pictures below. Read the message in the box. Write the message on the lines.

fish   I (me)   river

go   hungry   catch

These lines ‖ mean the end of a sentence.

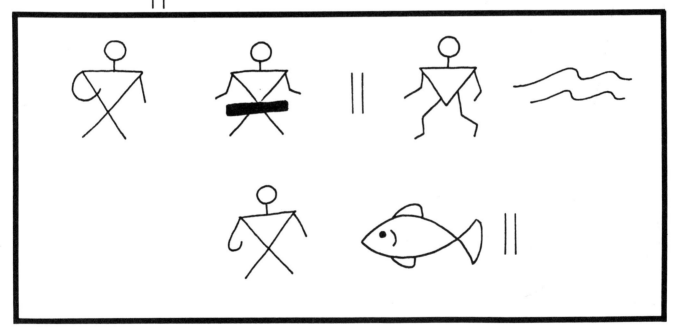

The message is: _____

_____

_____

Here are more Indian picture symbols. Use these – and the ones on the page before this one – to draw your own message. Write your message on the lines.

hunt

deer

rabbit

good

bad

eat

Here are more Indian picture symbols. Use them to read the story on the next page. You can also use them to write your own story on another piece of paper. Remember that these lines ‖ mean the end of a sentence.

Read the picture story. Write the story in words on another sheet of paper. Then use another piece of paper to draw your own story. Give it to a friend and have the friend read your story.

Indians drew picture symbols of the moon to show the time of year.

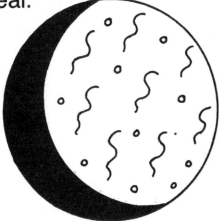

January: the snow moon

March: the month of the crow

July: the thunder moon

August: the corn moon

November: good month to hunt

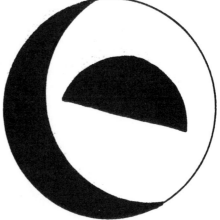

December: the month of long nights

Draw your own picture symbols to stand for the other months of the year.

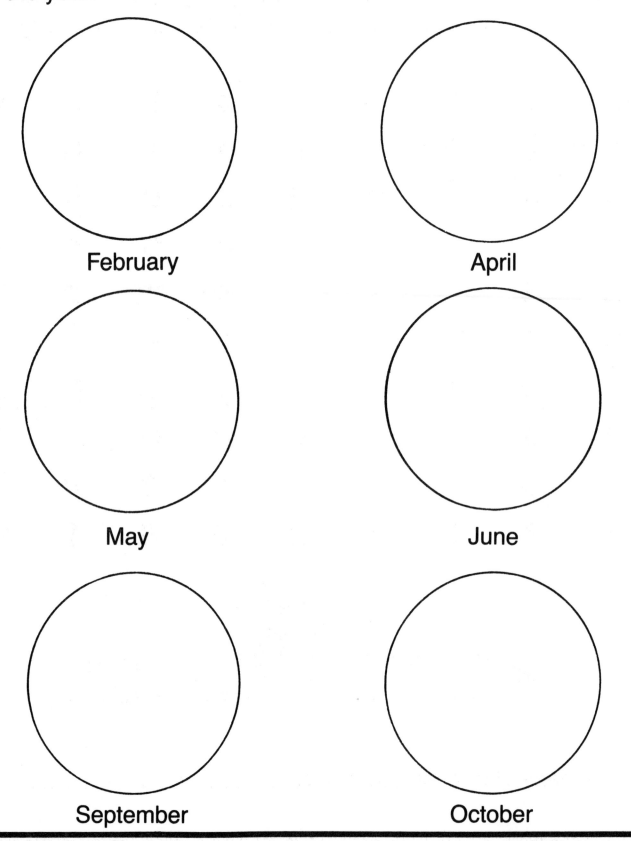

February

April

May

June

September

October

Spell as many words as you can by drawing lines from one letter to another. Do not draw a line through a letter unless it is in the word. Use each letter once. Two are done for you.

m	e	d	o	l	p	a	r	v
a	t	g	u	c	h	i	n	t
u	s	i	q	z	e	u	k	o
l	o	r	a	j	h	o	r	s
h	e	y	i	t	e	m	o	u
p	o	m	w	a	t	e	j	h
o	u	f	r	l	y	g	p	a
b	a	k	c	o	u	d	e	d
s	o	t	h	l	n	o	v	t
d	a	e	m	a	u	s	t	x

How many words did you find?_____

Spell as many words as you can by drawing lines from one letter to another. Do not draw a line through a letter unless it is in the word. Use each letter once.

x	o	y	e	p	u	s	t	e
r	t	j	o	y	a	l	k	u
i	q	t	e	i	c	m	a	r
z	u	a	o	k	h	e	i	w
b	e	d	s	a	z	i	o	c
m	a	r	p	n	u	e	d	i
o	f	h	r	o	s	t	a	l
k	x	a	u	p	v	i	n	d
n	o	b	y	q	g	a	t	e
i	t	a	e	u	a	c	k	n

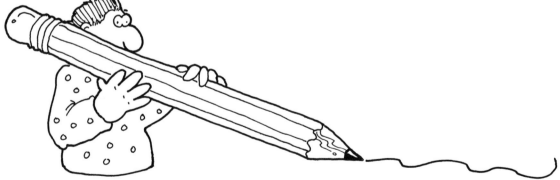

How many words did you find? _____

Rapunzel got tired of staying in the castle all day. She opened a new shop in town.

Draw a picture of what you think the witch will look like after Rapunzel fixes her hair!

Imagine that another fairy-tale or nursery-rhyme character gets a job or opens a store. What would the job be? What would the store sell? Draw a picture in the box.

It's fun to add a new verse to an old rhyme. Here is the old rhyme:

Little Miss Muffet
Sat on a tuffet,
Eating her curds and whey.
Along came a spider,
Who sat down beside her,
And frightened Miss Muffet away!

Here is the new rhyme:

Spidey thought he was lucky,
But the curds were so yucky,
He soon began to cry,
"Come back here, Miss Muffet,
You can keep your old tuffet.
I'd rather eat burgers and fries!"

Here's another old rhyme:

> Jack and Jill went up the hill,
> To fetch a pail of water.
> Jack fell down and broke his crown,
> And Jill came tumbling after.

Write a new verse to add to the old one. Then draw a picture of it.

_____

_____

_____

_____

_____

_____

Get another piece of paper and try this with some other rhymes!

When two small words fit together to make a bigger word, the new word is called a compound word. Use the words below to make as many compound words as you can. You can use the words more than once. One is done for you.

light	basket	lip	dog
house	candle	foot	boat
broom	moon	stick	ball

basketball

Put the words below together to make compound words. You can use each word more than once.

fire	gold	rain	star
coat	man	bird	bath
snow	bed	fish	room

_____   _____

_____   _____

_____   _____

_____   _____

_____   _____

_____   _____

_____   _____

Use the words below to make as many compound words as you can. You can use each word more than once.

night	down	bed	hand
town	hill	boy	up
back	stairs	time	paper

It's fun to draw words and make them look like what they mean.

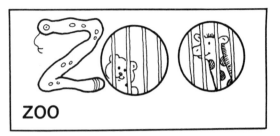

zoo

cloud

Choose one of the words below and draw it.

run	basket	happy	bump
hill	hair	bed	fat

Use another sheet of paper to draw some of the other words.

Choose three of the words below and draw them in the boxes. One is done for you.

circle	sad	train	pie
rope	dance	turn	jump
wave	hop	snake	people

rope

On another sheet of paper draw some more words. Use your own words, too!

A verb is an action word. It tells what someone or something does. A noun is a person, place, or thing. First, list all the verbs you can think of that tell what this dragon might do. Then go back and list nouns to go together with the verbs. The first two are done for you.

Verbs

eat

scare

Nouns

bugs

king

List all the verbs you can think of that tell what this robot might do. Then list nouns that go with the verbs. The first two are done for you.

Verbs

clean
fix

Nouns

house
cars

Remember that a noun is a person, place, or thing. List all the nouns that you might find inside Prince Dwayne's castle.

List all the nouns you might find inside Witch Margaret's cauldron.

Which letter is missing from each group of words? One is done for you. Fill in the letters to solve the riddle at the bottom of the page.

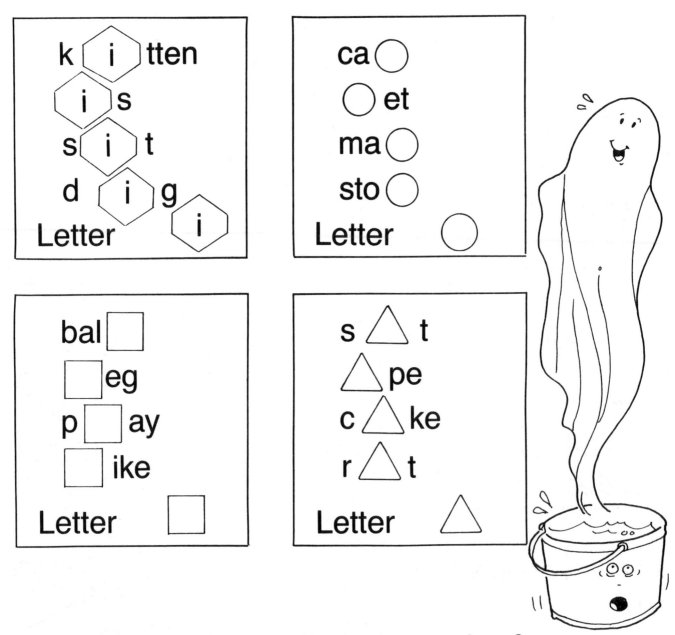

k ⬡(i) tten
(i) s
s (i) t
d (i) g
Letter ⬡(i)

ca ◯
◯ et
ma ◯
sto ◯
Letter ◯

bal ▢
▢ eg
p ▢ ay
▢ ike
Letter ▢

s △ t
△ pe
c △ ke
r △ t
Letter △

What do you call a bucket that just saw a ghost?

a pale   ◯ △ ⬡ ▢

Find the letter that is missing from each group of words. Then fill in the spaces and solve the riddle.

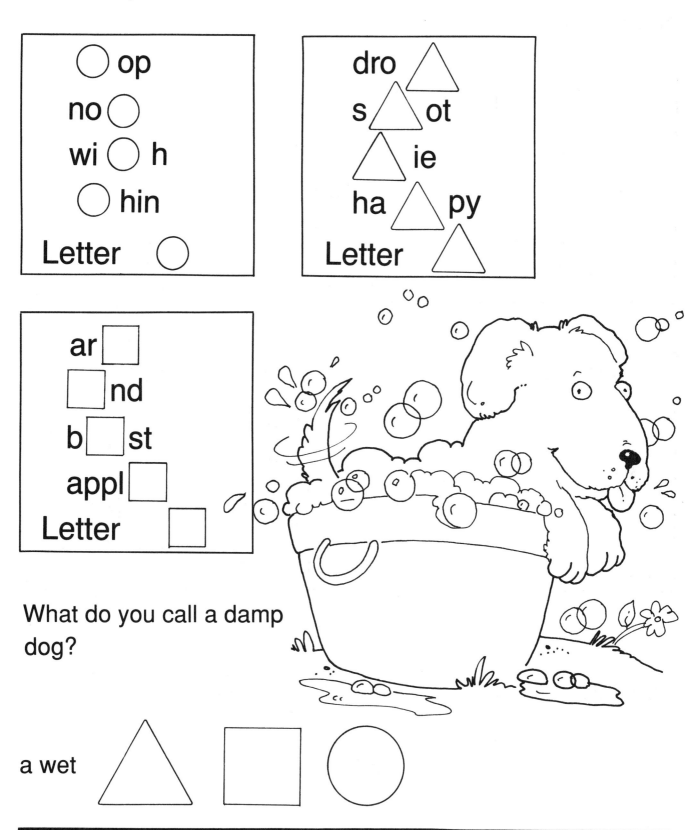

◯ op

no ◯

wi ◯ h

◯ hin

Letter ◯

dro △

s △ ot

△ ie

ha △ py

Letter △

ar ☐

☐ nd

b ☐ st

appl ☐

Letter ☐

What do you call a damp dog?

a wet △ ☐ ◯

Find the letter that is missing from each group of words.
Then fill in the spaces and solve the riddle.

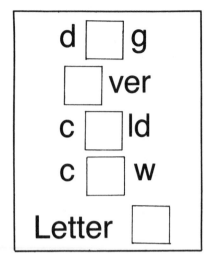

d ⬜ g
⬜ ver
c ⬜ ld
c ⬜ w
Letter ⬜

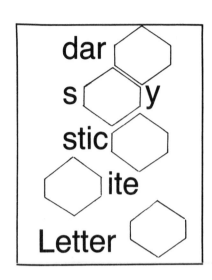

dar ⬡
s ⬡ y
stic ⬡
⬡ ite
Letter ⬡

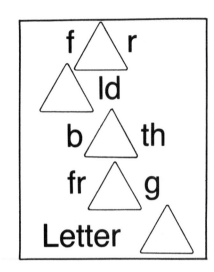

f △ r
△ ld
b △ th
fr △ g
Letter △

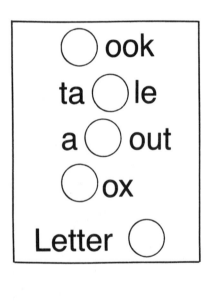

◯ ook
ta ◯ le
a ◯ out
◯ ox
Letter ◯

What do you call a person who steals stories?

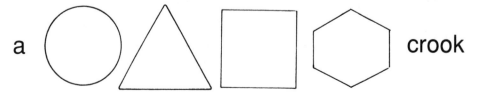

a ◯ △ ⬜ ⬡ crook

Find the letter that is missing from each group of words.
Then fill in the spaces and solve the riddle.

ye◯
fa◯t
◯ip
pu◯h

Letter ◯

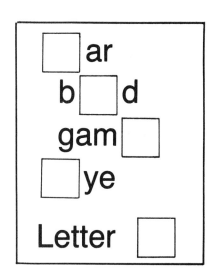

☐ar
b☐d
gam☐
☐ye

Letter ☐

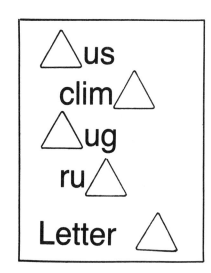

△us
clim△
△ug
ru△

Letter △

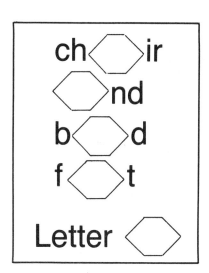

ch⬡ir
⬡nd
b⬡d
f⬡t

Letter ⬡

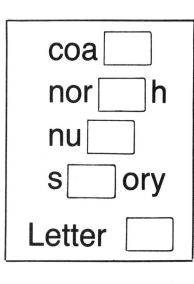

coa☐
nor☐h
nu☐
s☐ory

Letter ☐

What do you call a monster's dinner?

a △ ☐ ⬡ ◯ ☐ feast

Solve these word puzzles. The first one is done for you.

moøn + key =   monkey

1. ⬤ + 🌙 – m = _____

2. 🐷 – p + loo = _____

3. 🥧 – ie + 👂 = _____

Solve these word puzzles.

1.

g + 🏠 – use + ⭐ – ar =

_____

2.

🐪 – cam + ep + ✋ – d + t =

_____

3.

🦹 – ber + 🍲 – p =

_____

4.

🦇 – t + b + 🌙 – m =

_____

Make up your own word puzzles for the words below.

 = **horse**

 = **kangaroo**

 = **octopus**

Make up one of your own:

=

Finish the line drawings below. Then write a sentence about each picture. You can be silly or serious. With a little imagination, you can turn a line into anything! Two are done for you.

A ~~~~~ loves to eat leaves.

An 🍦 is good if it's chocolate.

_____ ∿∿∿ _____

_____ ⌒ _____

_____ ∿∿∿ _____

Finish the line drawings below. Then write a sentence about each picture.

This  is a Looney-Bird.

 _____

 _____

_____

_____

Homonyms are words that sound the same, but mean different things. Usually they are spelled differently, too. It's fun to put homonyms together and make funny pictures. Use the word box below to find the homonyms. Write each one under the correct picture.

meet - _____

_____ - won

bury - _____

_____ - prints

| one | prince | meat | win | berry | mate |

43

Draw your own silly homonym pictures.

pear - pair

eight - ate

flower - flour

Add as many words as you can to each list – by changing only one letter at a time. The first list has been started for you.

cat

hat

hot

hop

ball

Add as many words as you can to each list by changing only one letter at a time.

get

hand

The answer to the riddle is written in code. To read it you must cross out every other letter in each word. Write the answer on the lines below.

What did Jack's mother think when Jack told her what he got for selling their cow?

She thought Jack was:

fauolel opf bmeharnes

_____

_____

The answer to the riddle is written in code. To read it you must replace each letter with the letter that comes before it in the alphabet. That means that C changes to B, G changes to F, and so on. Write the answer on the lines below.

What did Daddy Cyclops say to Mommy Cyclops?

"J'mm lffq bo fzf po uif cbcz!"

He said:

"

!"

This code is called the Pig Pen code! Use it to read the answer to the riddle. Write the answer on the lines below.

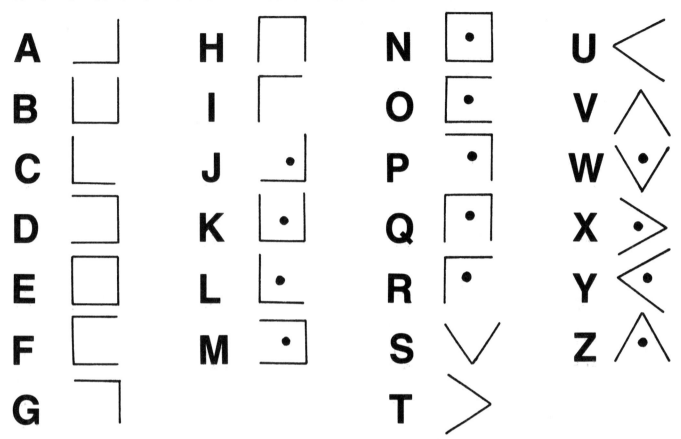

How did the fire fighter feel when her husband forgot her birthday?

She was:

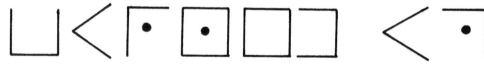

_____ _____

Choose one of the three codes that you used on pages 47, 48, and 49. Write your own coded message in the box. Get a friend to try to read it and write the message below.

The message is: _____

_____

_____

Match each car to the correct storybook character. One is done for you.

NO FAT

FIDLR3

NO YOLK

ZZZZZZ

Old King Cole

Sleeping Beauty

Jack Sprat

Humpty Dumpty

Match each car to the correct storybook character.

Captain Hook

Old Woman in a Shoe

Little Boy Blue

Georgie Porgie

Choose a storybook character or a real person. Make up a license plate for him or her. Use no more than 8 letters and numbers. Write the person's name on the line at the bottom of the page.

This car belongs to _____.

Dr. Dippo must write 4 names in her appointment book. Read **all** the clues below. Write each name in the correct place.

Monday: _____

Tuesday: _____

Wednesday: _____

Thursday: _____

Friday: _____

Saturday: _____

1. Susie's appointment is on Friday.

2. Gary's appointment is one day after Fred's.

3. Fred's appointment is two days before Don's.

4. Don's appointment is two days before Susie's.

Four children signed up for swimming lessons. Read all the clues below. Write each name in the correct place.

Monday: _____

Tuesday: _____

Wednesday: _____

Thursday: _____

Friday: _____

Saturday: _____

1. Angela swims on Thursday.

2. Jim swims three days before Lisa.

3. Rick swims two days after Angela.

4. Lisa swims the day before Rick.

Read the clues below. Fill in the schedule for the shows at Sea Park. Draw the clock hands, too!

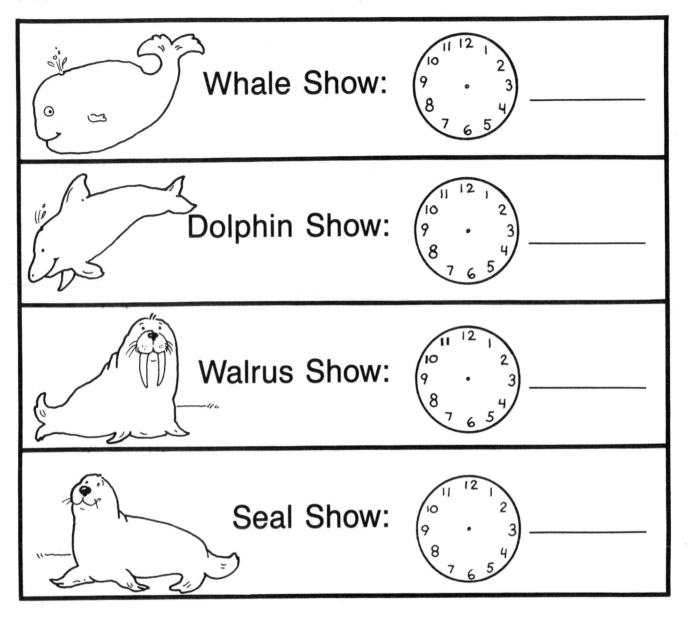

Whale Show: _____

Dolphin Show: _____

Walrus Show: _____

Seal Show: _____

1. The Walrus Show is at 3:30 P.M.

2. The whales perform 1 hour before the seals.

3. The Seal Show is 4 hours before the Walrus Show.

4. The dolphins perform 2½ hours after the seals.

Mix up compound words to make silly new ones! Use the word box below. Write your "crazy compounds" on the lines below and draw a picture of each one. One is done for you.

goldfish	mailbox	cheeseburger
eggshell	broomstick	treetop
hairbrush	junkyard	popcorn
snowman	seaweed	dishpan

goldfish + broomstick

broomfish

Make more crazy compounds! Use the compound words in the box below. You can also use the word box on page 57.

horseshoe	bedroom	rattlesnake
farmhouse	butterfly	moonlight
football	bathtub	scarecrow
arrowhead	starfish	spaceship

_____

_____

_____

Read this Good Luck — Bad Luck story.

1. What good luck!
   The bears were out.

2. What bad luck!
   One bear went out too far.

3. What good luck!
   He was friendly.

4. What bad luck!
   He was **too** friendly.

5. What good luck!
   He was ticklish.

Write your own Good Luck — Bad Luck story. Draw pictures for it.

1. What good luck!

_____

_____

2. What bad luck!

_____

_____

3. What good luck!

_____

_____

4. What bad luck!

_____

_____

5. What good luck!

_____

_____

Use the word box to fill in the empty squares. One is done for you.

Word Box

flag	thing	ring	roll
top	want	thin	stop
water	cake	sled	cap

61

Use the word box to fill in the empty squares. Make words
that go across and down. One is done for you.

A.

b
e
e g g

B.

r

C.

k

D.

o

Word Box

ride	kite	bee	kings
pot	egg	box	skate
red	car	lake	bed

Use the word box to fill in the word grid. The words must go across and down. One is done for you.

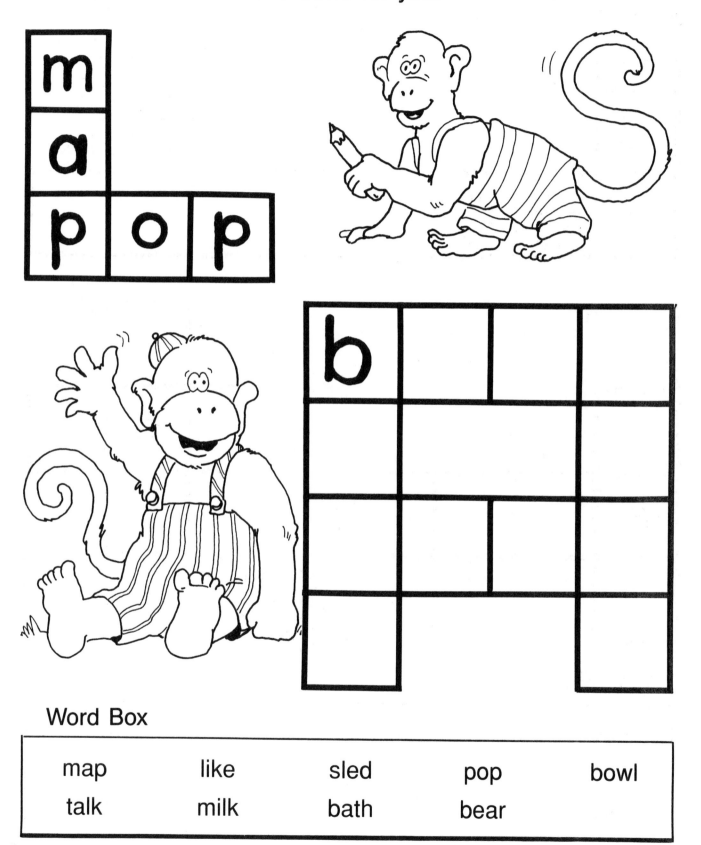

Word Box

map	like	sled	pop	bowl
talk	milk	bath	bear	

Fill in the empty squares to make words. You may use another piece of paper for practice.

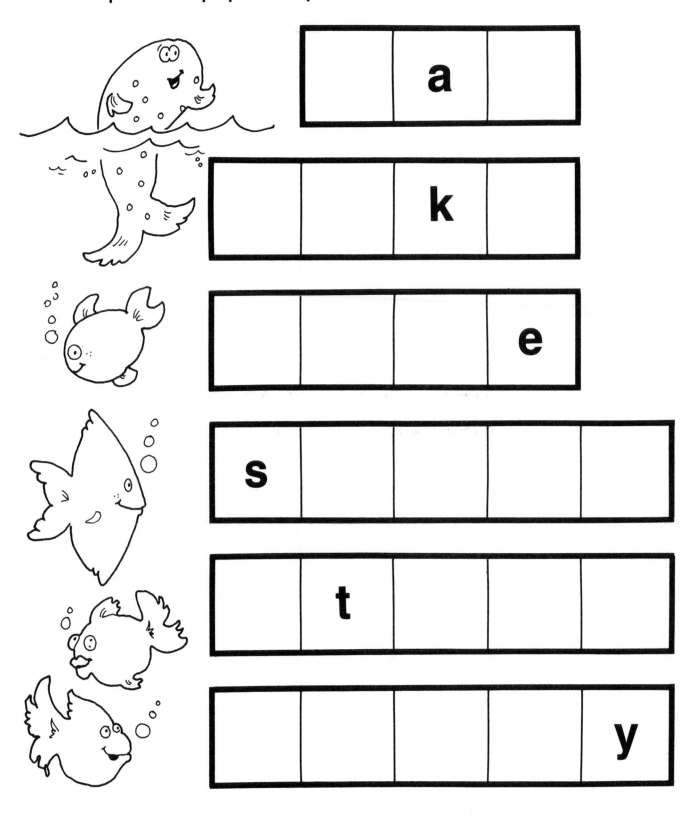

	a	

		k	

			e

s				

	t			

				y

Fill in the empty squares to make words that go across and down. It's a good idea to try out your words on another piece of paper.

Fill in the word grids with words that go across and down.
Don't use any word more than once.

66

Fill in the word grids with words that go across and down. Don't use any word more than once.

Use the letters in this square to make as many words as you can. Two are done for you. You may need to use more paper.

sat

rose

How many words did you find? _____

Read this "Recipe for a Fall Day."

Ingredients:

24 cups of sunshine

2 small clouds

3 lumps of fresh air

10 tons of falling leaves

1 bunch of children

Directions:

1. Paint leaves red, yellow, orange, and brown.

2. Bake leaves in sunshine until they are dry and crunchy.

3. Add children to leaves. Stir.

Write a recipe for something you **don't** eat — a party, a rainbow, a summer vacation, or anything you can think of!

My Recipe for _____

Ingredients: _____

_____

_____

_____

Directions: _____

_____

_____

_____

_____

Draw a picture of what it looks like when it's all done.

Use the words below to write as many sentences as you can. Be silly or serious! You may need more paper. One is done for you.

I	dog	want
monster	to	big
a	have	and

I have a dog.

_____

_____

_____

_____

_____

_____

_____

How many sentences did you write? _____

Use the words below to write as many sentences as you can. You may need more paper.

and	to	come	tree
we	robot	she	was
the	fast	a	not
over	will	apple	eat

_____

_____

_____

_____

_____

_____

How many sentences did you write? _____

Everything is always **wrong** in Looneyville. The Loonies like it that way! Today the mayor is upset because there are some things that are **right** in Looneyville! Find and circle 10 things that are **right** on this page and page 74.

If one storybook character sent a valentine to another character, it might look like this:

Dear Tink,

You are the light of my life.

Love,
Peter

Here is another make-believe valentine from a real person who lived a long time ago:

Dear Martha,

I cannot tell a lie. I love you.

Love,
George

Write a valentine from a storybook character or a person who lived long ago.

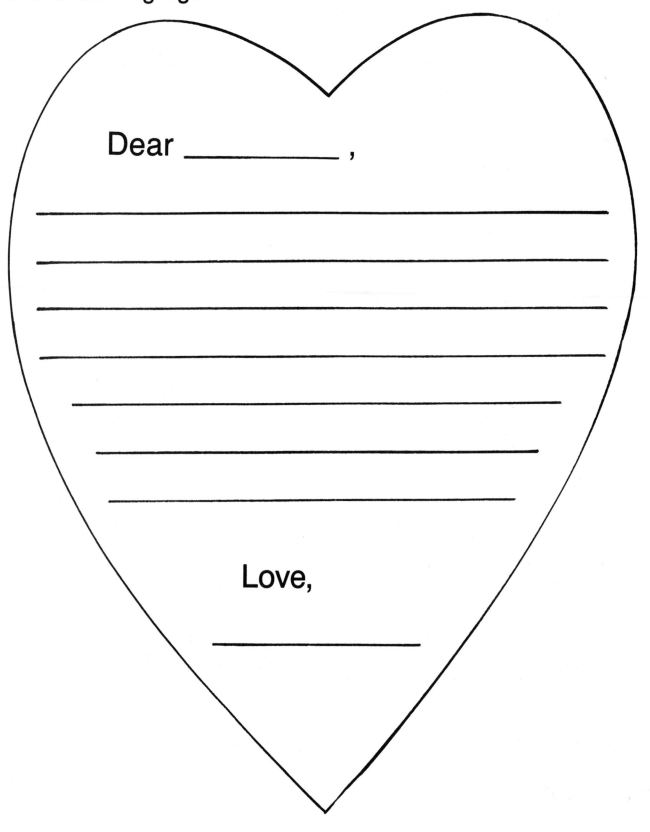

Dear _____ ,

Love,

Samuel Morse invented this famous code. Use the Morse Code to find the answer to the riddle below. Write the answer on the line at the bottom of the page.

Morse Code

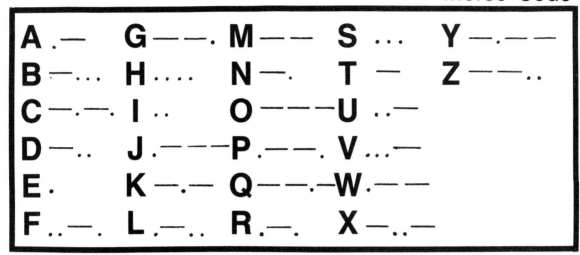

A .—	G ——.	M ——	S ...	Y —.——
B —...	H	N —.	T —	Z ——..
C —.—.	I ..	O ———	U ..—	
D —..	J .———	P .——.	V ...—	
E .	K —.—	Q ——.—	W .——	
F ..—.	L .—..	R .—.	X —..—	

What does the Gingerbread Boy use to make his bed?

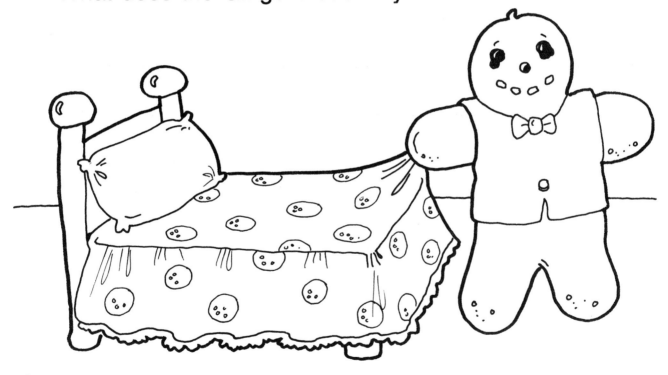

—.—.   ———   ———   —.—   ..   .   .   —

He uses a _____ .

Use the Morse Code to decode the answer to this riddle:

What did the mommy skunk say to the baby skunk?

-.-- --- ..-   .- .-. .

--- -.. --- .-. .- -... .-.. .

She said: "_____

_____!"

This code is called Trevanion's Code. To find the secret message in this letter, you must circle every **third** word after a **punctuation** mark. The first word is done for you.

Dear Jane,

We will (meet) again next Friday. Judy and Max will be there. So be at my house on time, and by midnight the meeting will be over.

Rocky

The secret message is:

Meet

To read the answer to the riddle below, you must replace each letter with the letter that comes **after** it in the alphabet. C becomes D, S becomes T, and so on. Write the answer on the line.

What do penguins like to ride?

Answer: h b d b x b k d r

They ride on _____ .

Here is a Box Code. To decode the message, you must read the letters in the box from left to right. The first one is done for you.

M	y	d	o
g	h	a	s
t	e	n	f
l	e	a	s

The message is:

My dog has ten fleas.

Find the message below. Write it on the lines.

T	h	r	e	e
m	o	n	s	t
e	r	s	a	r
e	b	e	h	i
n	d	y	o	u

Make up a message in Box Code. Your message must have 36 letters. Write it in the box below. Give it to a friend and see if he or she can decode it!

The secret message is: _____

_____

_____

_____

This is the Typewriter code. Use it to find the answer to the riddle. Write the answer on the line below.

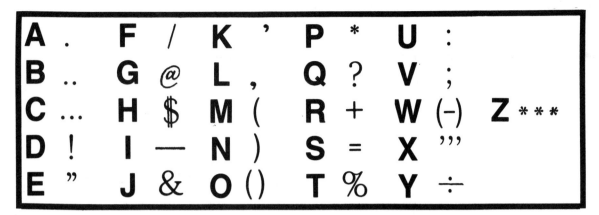

A	.	F	/	K	'	P	*	U	:		
B	..	G	@	L	,	Q	?	V	;		
C	...	H	$	M	(	R	+	W	(-)	Z	***
D	!	I	—	N	)	S	=	X	'''		
E	"	J	&	O	()	T	%	Y	÷		

What do you get when you cross a chicken with a bell?

Answer: •)   • , • + (••• , : ••• '

You get _____ .

Use the word box to help you fill in the word pyramid. One word is done for you.

Word Box

star	so	saw	story	was
lions	best	is	stones	

84

Use the word box to help you fill in the word pyramid.

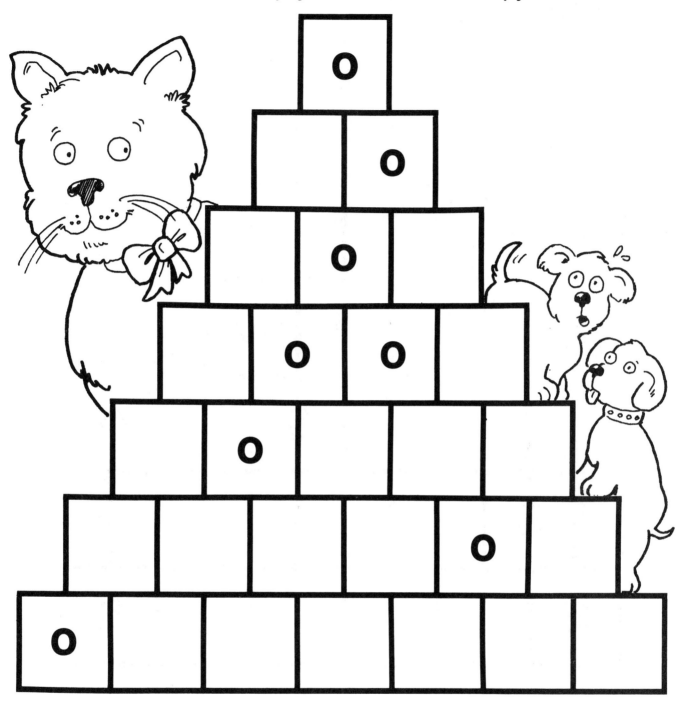

Word Box

window	look	on	over	socks
most	no	outside	box	

Fill in the word pyramid with 5 words.

You need 10 words to fill in this big word pyramid!

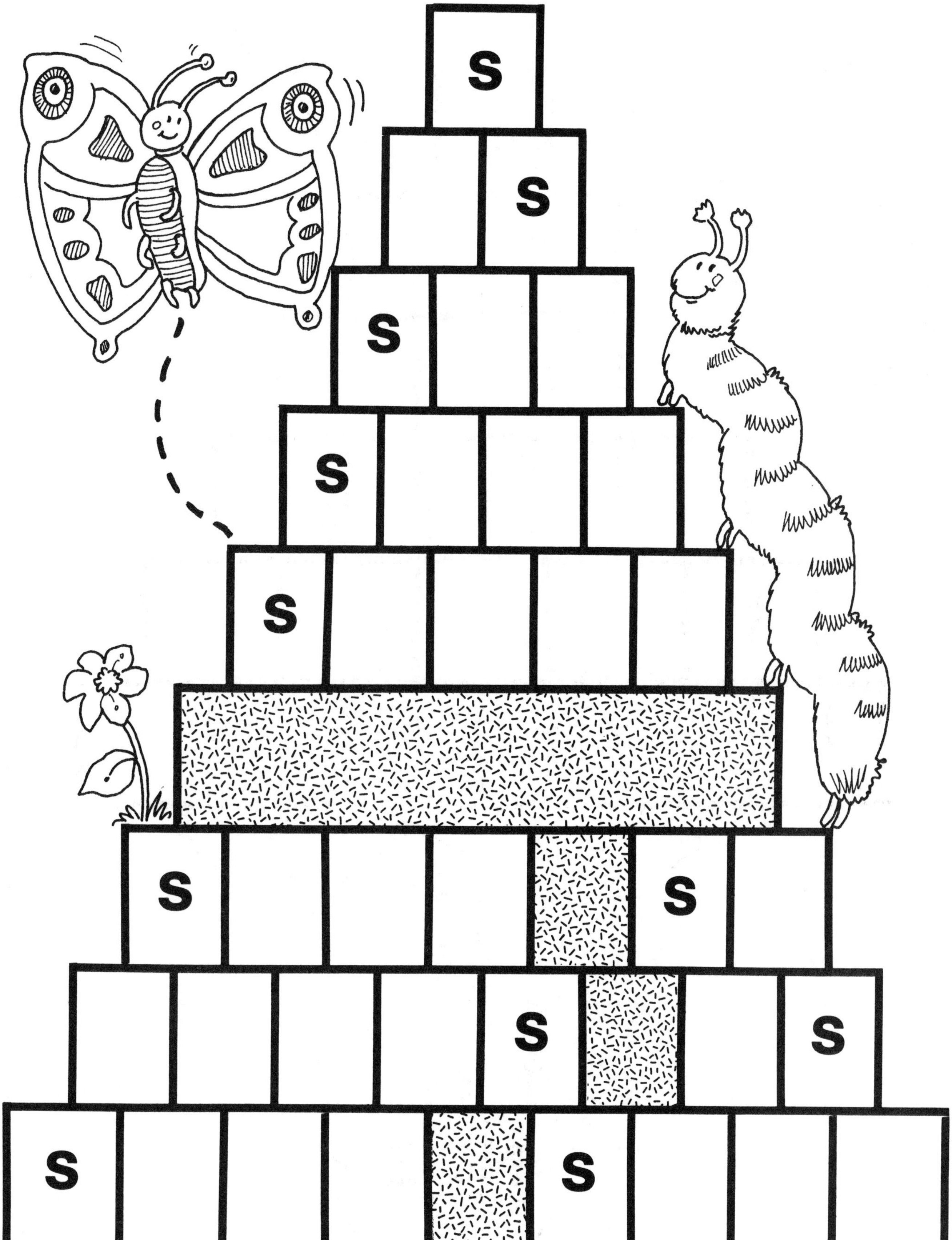

S

S

S

S

S

S

S

S

S

S

Fill in this word pyramid with 10 words. Use as many letter a's as you can.

How many a's are in your pyramid? _____

Look at the words on the dial. Close your eyes. Move your finger around the dial. Stop. Open your eyes. Write the word you stopped on. Do it again. Draw a picture of one thing that your two words tell about. On this page one is done for you.

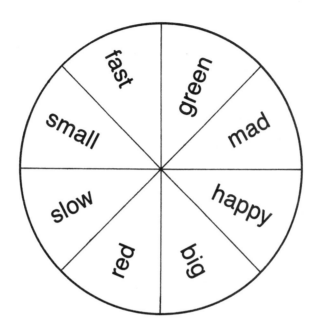

Here is something ___fast___ and ___green___.
It is __a pickle on his way to a picnic.__.

89

Use the dial on the page before. Write your words below.
Draw your pictures.

1. Here is something _____ and _____ .

It is a _____

_____ .

2. Here is something _____ and _____ .

It is a _____

_____ .

Draw a picture in each box. The first one is done for you.

Did you ever see . . .

. . . a hot dog?

. . . a home run?

. . . a soda pop?

. . . time fly?

Draw a picture in each box.

Did you ever see . . .

. . . a banana split?

. . . a hat box?

. . . a wrist watch?

. . . a jelly roll?

List things you can change by making them bigger. Two are done for you.

Make it bigger and change a . . .

<u>coffee cup</u>   into   <u>a swimming pool</u>

<u>fork</u>   into   <u>a rake</u>

_____ into _____

_____ into _____

_____ into _____

_____ into _____

_____ into _____

_____ into _____

_____ into _____

List things you can change by making them smaller. Two are done for you.

Make it smaller and change a . . .

helicopter	into	a fan
blanket	into	a napkin
_____	into	_____
_____	into	_____
_____	into	_____
_____	into	_____
_____	into	_____
_____	into	_____
_____	into	_____

Page 7:   JUMP

Page 8:   MARCH

Page 9:   SPLASH

Page 10: PIRATE

Page 11: CANDY

Page 12: DRIVE

Page 13: I'm hungry. I will go to the river to catch a fish.

Page 16: I hiked up the mountains with my friends. The mountains were cold.
I was happy to hike down the mountains!

Page 25: basketball, football, stickball, boathouse, broomstick, candlestick,
moonlight, footlight, lipstick, doghouse, houseboat (You may find other
words, too.)

Page 26: fireman, firebird, snowbird, snowman, raincoat, bedroom, coatroom,
starfish, bathroom, goldfish (You may find other words, too.)

Page 27: downtown, downhill, uphill, uptown, paperboy, paperback, upstairs,
backstairs, nighttime, bedtime, backhand, downstairs (You may find other
words, too.)

Page 34: pail

Page 35: pet

Page 36: book

Page 37: beast

Page 38: 1. balloon 2. igloo 3. pear

Page 39: 1. ghost 2. elephant 3. robot 4. baboon

Page 43: meet-meat, one-won, bury-berry, prince-prints

Page 47: full of beans

Page 48: "I'll keep an eye on the baby!"

Page 49: burned up

Page 54: Monday: Fred   Page 55: Tuesday: Jim
Tuesday: Gary   Thursday: Angela
Wednesday: Don   Friday: Lisa
Friday: Susie   Saturday: Rick

Page 56: Whale Show: 10:30 A.M.   Page 61: top
Dolphin Show: 2:00 P.M.   want
Walrus Show: 3:30 P.M.   cake
Seal Show: 11:30 A.M.   thing

Page 62: B. car, ride C. lake, kite D. box, pot

Page 63: b o w l
         a   i
         t a l k
         h   e

Page 77: cookie sheet

Page 78: "You are odorable!"

Page 79: Meet Max at midnight.

Page 80: icecycles

Page 81: Three monsters are behind you.

Page 83: an alarm cluck

Page 84: so   Page 85: no
saw   box
best   look
story   socks
stones   window
                             outside